**Editor in Chief**
Ina Massler Levin, M.A.

**Editor**
Eric Migliaccio

**Contributing Editor**
Sarah Smith

**Creative Director**
Karen J. Goldfluss, M.S. Ed.

**Cover Design**
Tony Carrillo / Marilyn Goldberg

*Teacher Created Resources, Inc.*
6421 Industry Way
Westminster, CA 92683
www.teachercreated.com
**ISBN: 978-1-4206-5913-9**

*©2010 Teacher Created Resources, Inc.*
Reprinted, 2011 (PO4838)
Made in U.S.A.

This book belongs to

_____

Ready·Set·Learn

# Get Ready to Learn!

Get ready, get set, and go!  Boost your child's learning with this exciting series of books.  Geared to help children practice and master many needed skills, the Ready·Set·Learn books are bursting with 64 pages of learning fun.  Use these books for . . .

* enrichment
* skills reinforcement
* extra practice

With their smaller size, the Ready·Set·Learn books fit easily in children's hands, backpacks, and book bags.  All your child needs to get started are pencils, crayons, and colored pencils.

A full sheet of colorful stickers is included.  Use these stickers for . . .

* decorating pages
* rewarding outstanding effort
* keeping track of completed pages

Celebrate your child's progress by using these stickers on the reward chart located on the inside cover.  The blue-ribbon sticker fits perfectly on the certificate on page 64.

With Ready·Set·Learn and a little encouragement, your child will be on the fast track to learning fun!

# Identifying Parts

**Directions:** Count the number of parts.

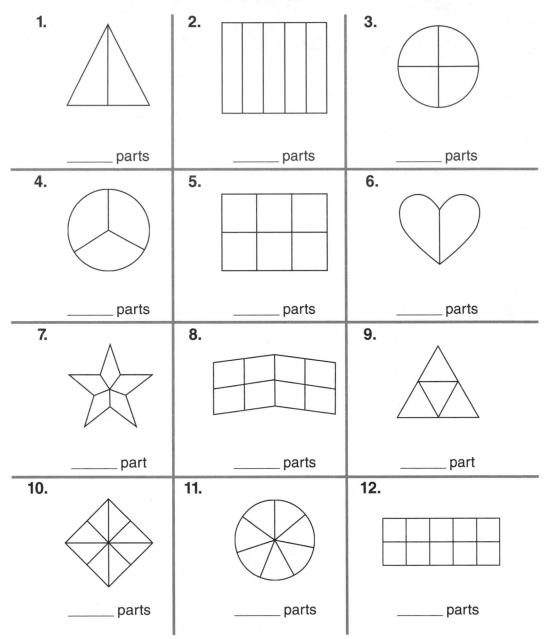

1.

_____ parts

2.

_____ parts

3.

_____ parts

4.

_____ parts

5.

_____ parts

6.

_____ parts

7.

_____ part

8.

_____ parts

9.

_____ part

10.

_____ parts

11.

_____ parts

12.

_____ parts

4

# Identifying Shaded Parts

**Directions:** How many parts are shaded? Write the number.

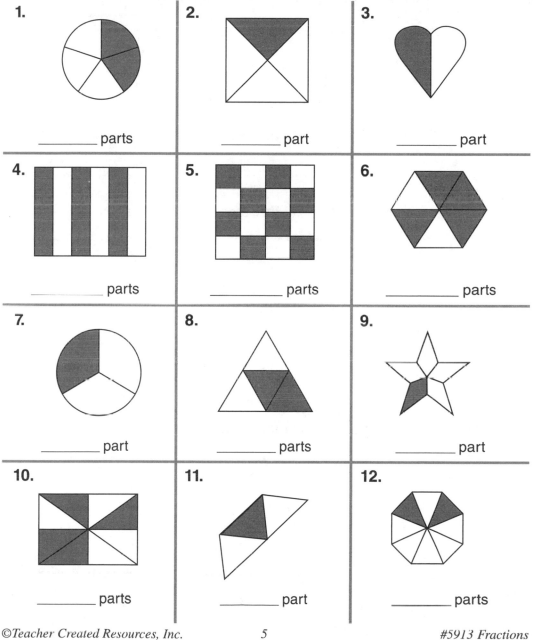

1. _____ parts

2. _____ part

3. _____ part

4. _____ parts

5. _____ parts

6. _____ parts

7. _____ part

8. _____ parts

9. _____ part

10. _____ parts

11. _____ part

12. _____ parts

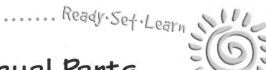

# Draw Equal Parts

**Directions:** Draw a line to show **two equal parts.**

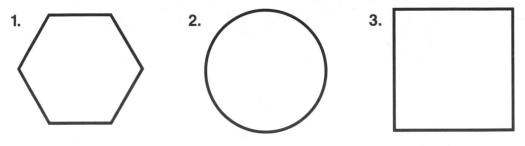

1.

2.

3.

**Directions:** Draw lines to show **three equal parts**.

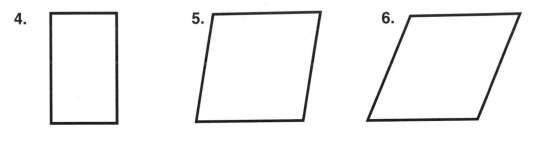

4.

5.

6.

**Directions:** Draw lines to show **four equal parts**.

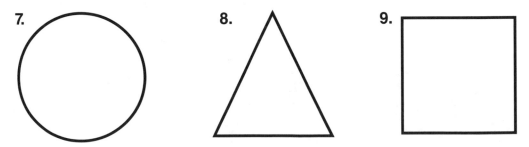

7.

8.

9.

# Identifying Equal Parts

**Directions:** Circle *yes* if the parts are equal. Circle *no* if the parts are not equal.

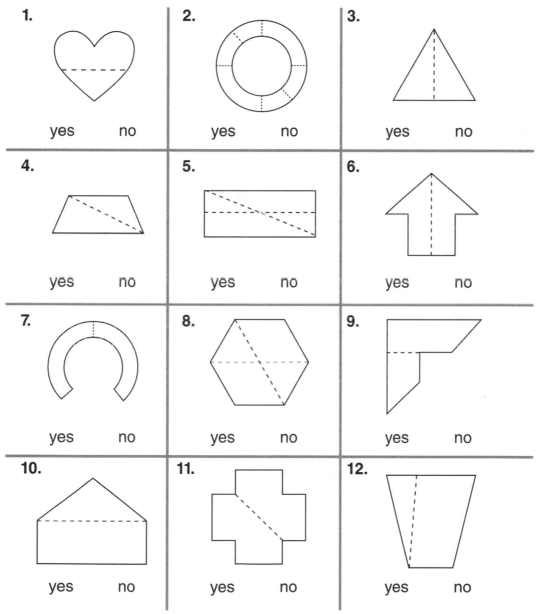

1.

yes     no

2.

yes     no

3.

yes     no

4.

yes     no

5.

yes     no

6.

yes     no

7.

yes     no

8.

yes     no

9.

yes     no

10.

yes     no

11.

yes     no

12.

yes     no

# Identifying Equal Parts

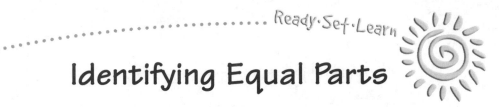

**Directions:** Read each question. Then circle the correct shapes.

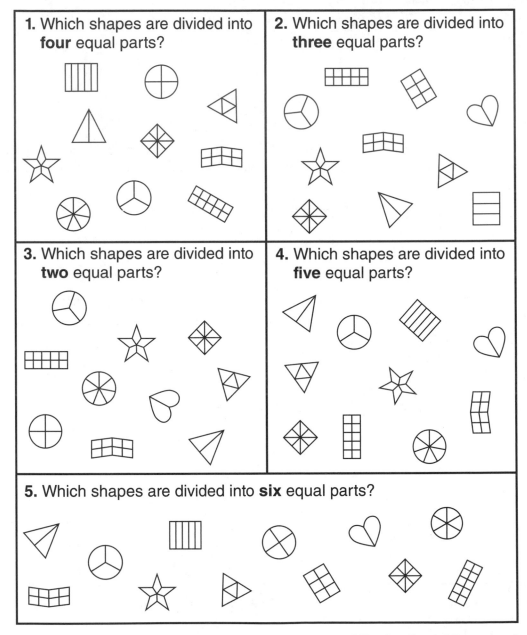

**1.** Which shapes are divided into **four** equal parts?

**2.** Which shapes are divided into **three** equal parts?

**3.** Which shapes are divided into **two** equal parts?

**4.** Which shapes are divided into **five** equal parts?

**5.** Which shapes are divided into **six** equal parts?

# Writing Numerators

**Directions:** Look at the shapes below. Parts of each shape are shaded. Write the number of parts shaded for each shape in the box at the top of each fraction. This number is called the *numerator*. The first one has already been done for you.

**1.**

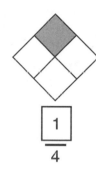

$$\frac{1}{4}$$

**2.**

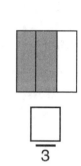

$$\frac{\phantom{0}}{3}$$

**3.**

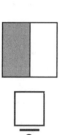

$$\frac{\phantom{0}}{2}$$

**4.**

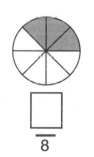

$$\frac{\phantom{0}}{8}$$

**5.**

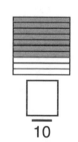

$$\frac{\phantom{0}}{10}$$

**6.**

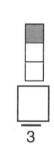

$$\frac{\phantom{0}}{3}$$

**7.**

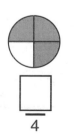

$$\frac{\phantom{0}}{4}$$

**8.**

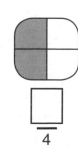

$$\frac{\phantom{0}}{4}$$

**9.**

$$\frac{\phantom{0}}{6}$$

# Coloring Fractions

**Directions:** Color the correct part of each shape to match the fraction. The first one has been done for you.

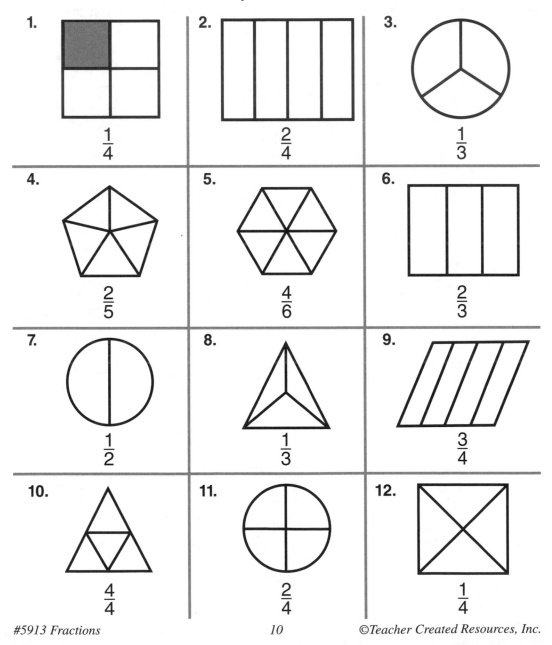

1.

$\dfrac{1}{4}$

2.

$\dfrac{2}{4}$

3.

$\dfrac{1}{3}$

4.

$\dfrac{2}{5}$

5.

$\dfrac{4}{6}$

6.

$\dfrac{2}{3}$

7.

$\dfrac{1}{2}$

8.

$\dfrac{1}{3}$

9.

$\dfrac{3}{4}$

10.

$\dfrac{4}{4}$

11.

$\dfrac{2}{4}$

12.

$\dfrac{1}{4}$

# One-Thirds

**Directions:** These pods have 3 equal-sized peas. Color the correct number of peas for each fraction.

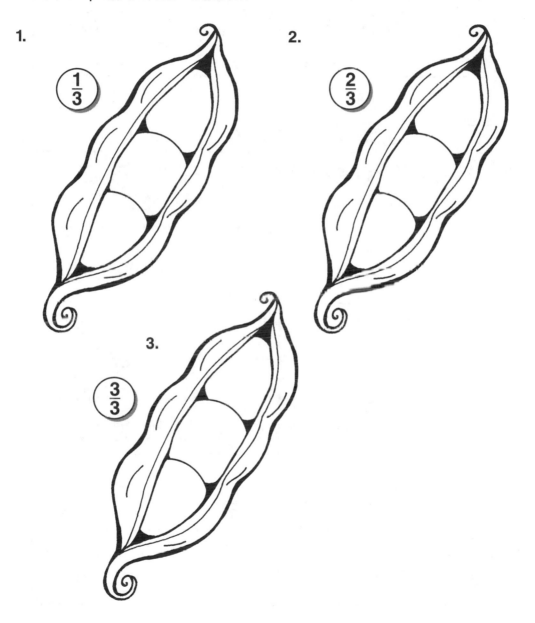

1.

$\frac{1}{3}$

2.

$\frac{2}{3}$

3.

$\frac{3}{3}$

# Identifying Shaded Parts

**Directions:** Write the number of shaded circles in the box.

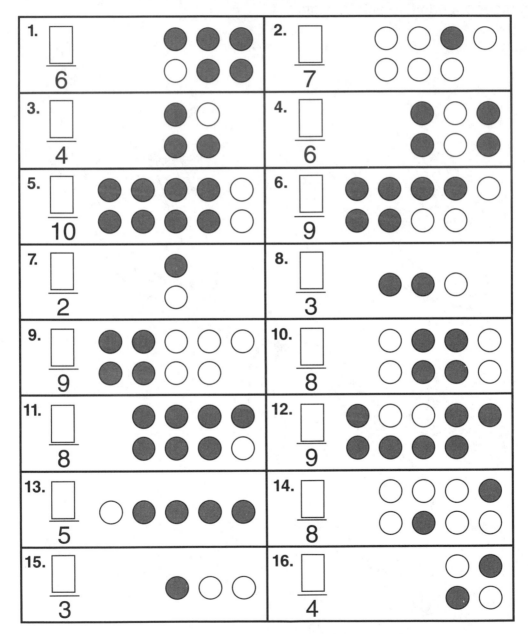

# Writing Fractions

**Directions:** Look at each shape. Write the fraction that tells how many parts of the whole object are shaded. The first one has already been done for you.

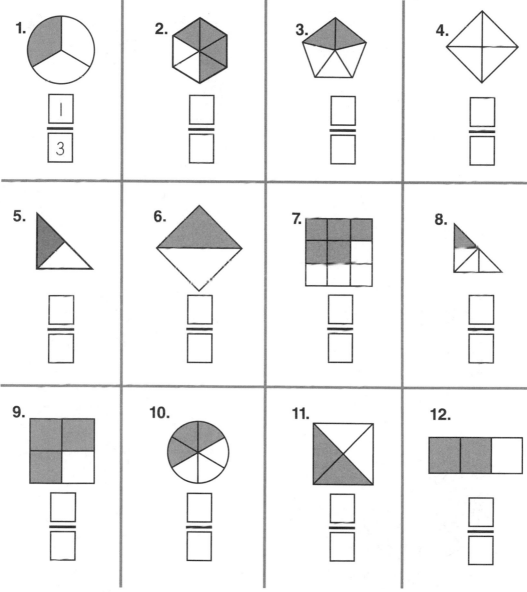

1. $\dfrac{1}{3}$

# Pizza, Pizza!

**Directions:** Look at the pizzas in the column on the left. Find the missing slices in the column on the right. Draw a line from the pizzas on the left to the correct number of pizza slices on the right.

**1.**

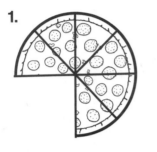

**a.**

**2.**

**b.**

**3.**

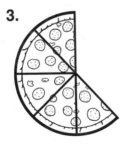

**c.**

**4.**

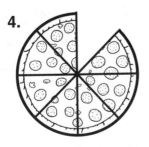

**d.**

# Fraction Practice

**Directions:** Follow the directions in each box.

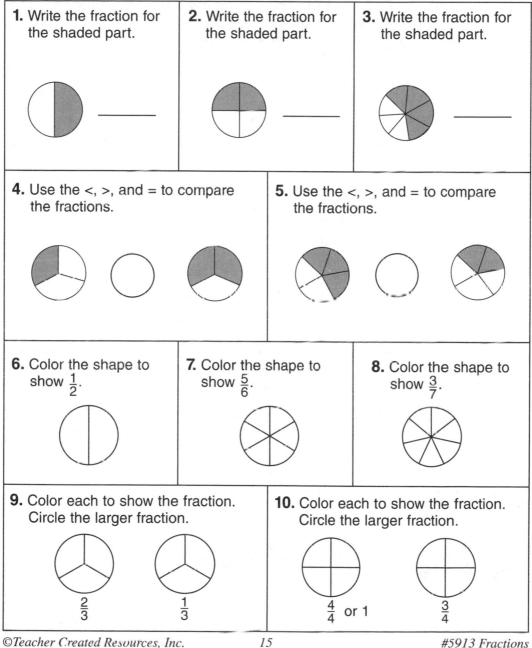

1. Write the fraction for the shaded part.

2. Write the fraction for the shaded part.

3. Write the fraction for the shaded part.

4. Use the <, >, and = to compare the fractions.

5. Use the <, >, and = to compare the fractions.

6. Color the shape to show $\frac{1}{2}$.

7. Color the shape to show $\frac{5}{6}$.

8. Color the shape to show $\frac{3}{7}$.

9. Color each to show the fraction. Circle the larger fraction.

$\frac{2}{3}$    $\frac{1}{3}$

10. Color each to show the fraction. Circle the larger fraction.

$\frac{4}{4}$ or 1    $\frac{3}{4}$

# Writing Fractions

**Directions:** The top number of the fraction is the **numerator**. It tells how many parts are needed or used. The bottom number of the fraction is the **denominator**. It tells the total number of parts. Write the fraction that tells how many are shaded. The first one is done for you.

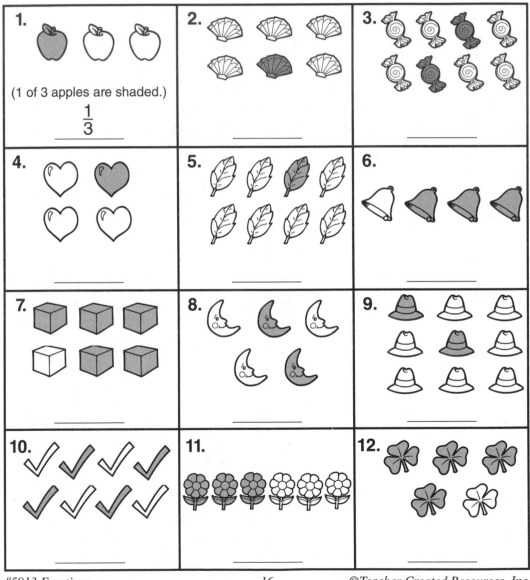

# More Fraction Practice

**Directions:** Follow the directions given in each box.

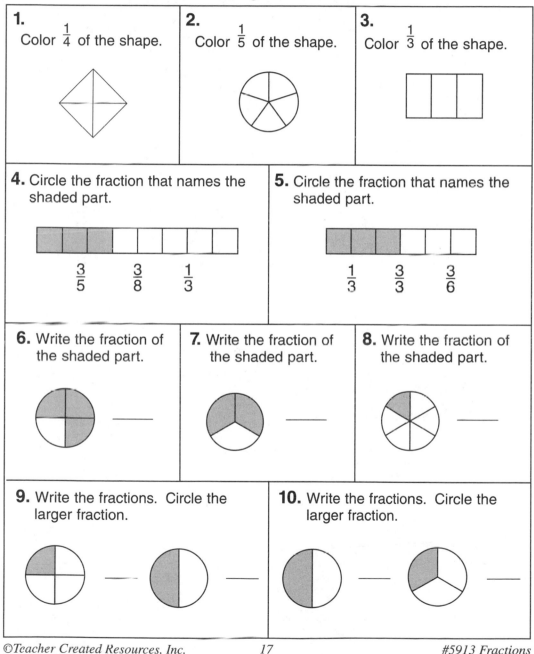

**1.**
Color $\frac{1}{4}$ of the shape.

**2.**
Color $\frac{1}{5}$ of the shape.

**3.**
Color $\frac{1}{3}$ of the shape.

**4.** Circle the fraction that names the shaded part.

$\frac{3}{5}$   $\frac{3}{8}$   $\frac{1}{3}$

**5.** Circle the fraction that names the shaded part.

$\frac{1}{3}$   $\frac{3}{3}$   $\frac{3}{6}$

**6.** Write the fraction of the shaded part.

**7.** Write the fraction of the shaded part.

**8.** Write the fraction of the shaded part.

**9.** Write the fractions. Circle the larger fraction.

**10.** Write the fractions. Circle the larger fraction.

# Name the Fraction

**Directions:** Write a fraction for each picture. The first one has been done for you.

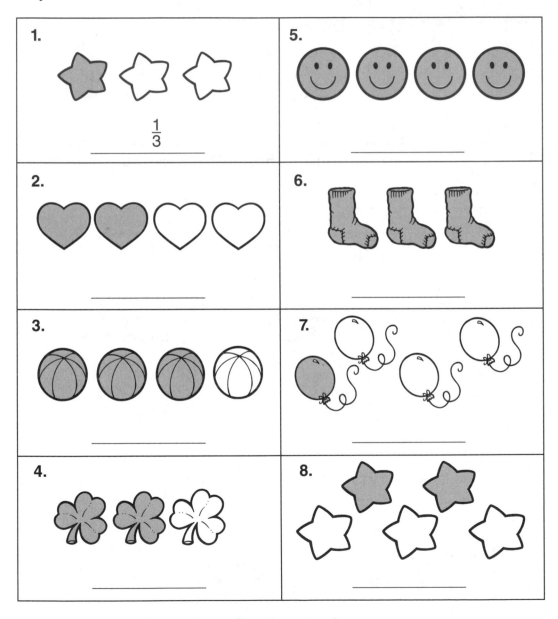

1.

$\frac{1}{3}$
_____

5.

_____

2.

_____

6.

_____

3.

_____

7.

_____

4.

_____

8.

_____

# Parts of a Whole

**Directions:** What part of each shape is shaded? Draw a line to the correct fraction.

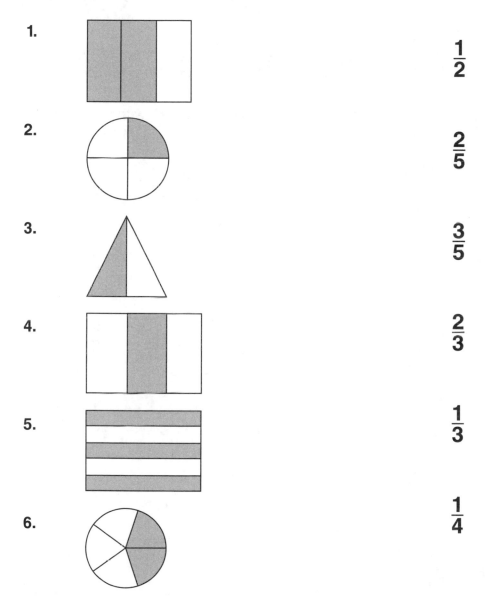

1.

2.

3.

4.

5.

6.

$\dfrac{1}{2}$

$\dfrac{2}{5}$

$\dfrac{3}{5}$

$\dfrac{2}{3}$

$\dfrac{1}{3}$

$\dfrac{1}{4}$

# A Part of the Whole

A *fraction* is a part of a whole. If you had a pizza for dinner and the pizza was cut into 8 equal slices, each slice would represent $\frac{1}{8}$ of the pizza. It would take 8 $\frac{1}{8}$'s to make a whole pizza.

**Directions:** Draw a line to match the correct picture with the fraction that represents the picture.

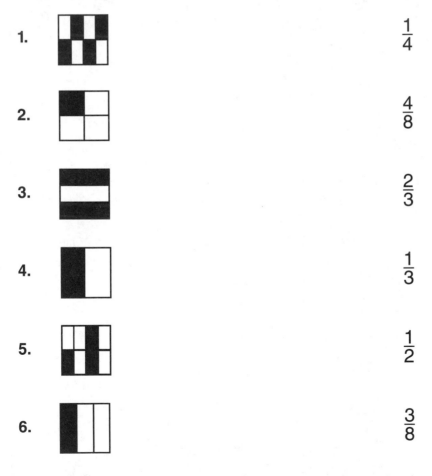

1.                                     $\frac{1}{4}$

2.                                     $\frac{4}{8}$

3.                                     $\frac{2}{3}$

4.                                     $\frac{1}{3}$

5.                                     $\frac{1}{2}$

6.                                     $\frac{3}{8}$

                      20                      

# Identifying Parts of a Whole and Parts of a Set

**Directions:** Follow the directions given in each box.

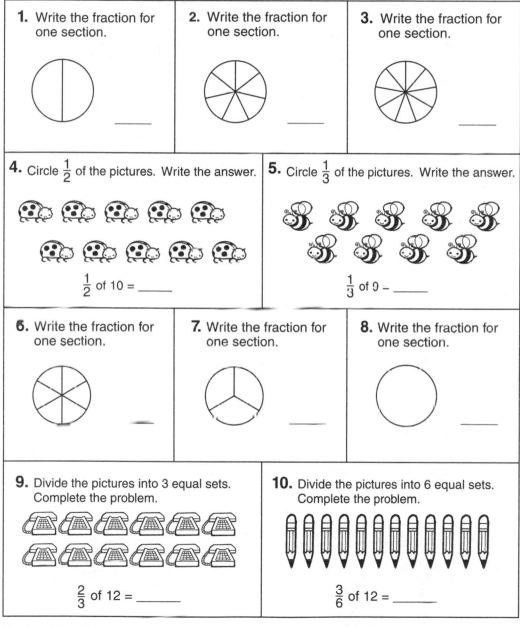

1. Write the fraction for one section. _____

2. Write the fraction for one section. _____

3. Write the fraction for one section. _____

4. Circle $\frac{1}{2}$ of the pictures. Write the answer.

$\frac{1}{2}$ of 10 = _____

5. Circle $\frac{1}{3}$ of the pictures. Write the answer.

$\frac{1}{3}$ of 9 – _____

6. Write the fraction for one section. _____

7. Write the fraction for one section. _____

8. Write the fraction for one section. _____

9. Divide the pictures into 3 equal sets. Complete the problem.

$\frac{2}{3}$ of 12 = _____

10. Divide the pictures into 6 equal sets. Complete the problem.

$\frac{3}{6}$ of 12 = _____

# Matching Fractions

**Directions:** Match each set of pictures to the correct fraction.

$$\frac{1}{2}$$

$$\frac{1}{4}$$

$$\frac{1}{3}$$

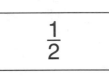

# Writing Fractions

**Directions:** Write the fraction two ways—using numbers and words.

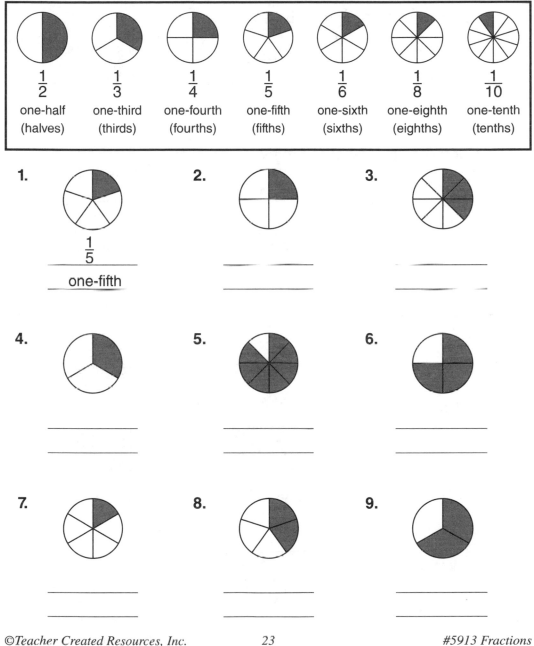

| $\frac{1}{2}$ | $\frac{1}{3}$ | $\frac{1}{4}$ | $\frac{1}{5}$ | $\frac{1}{6}$ | $\frac{1}{8}$ | $\frac{1}{10}$ |
|---|---|---|---|---|---|---|
| one-half (halves) | one-third (thirds) | one-fourth (fourths) | one-fifth (fifths) | one-sixth (sixths) | one-eighth (eighths) | one-tenth (tenths) |

1.
$$\frac{1}{5}$$
one-fifth

2.

3.

4.

5.

6.

7.

8.

9.

# Beginning Fractions

**Directions:** Read and follow each set of directions.

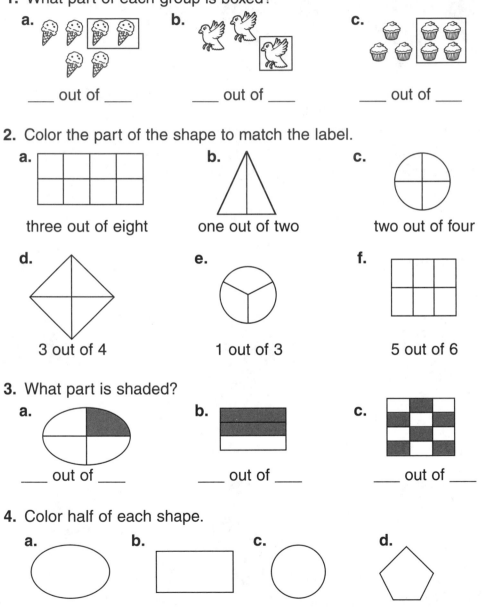

1. What part of each group is boxed?

   **a.**                    **b.**                              **c.**

   ___ out of ___            ___ out of ___                     ___ out of ___

2. Color the part of the shape to match the label.

   **a.**                    **b.**                    **c.**

   three out of eight        one out of two            two out of four

   **d.**                    **e.**                    **f.**

   3 out of 4                1 out of 3                5 out of 6

3. What part is shaded?

   **a.**                    **b.**                    **c.**

   ___ out of ___            ___ out of ___            ___ out of ___

4. Color half of each shape.

   **a.**          **b.**          **c.**          **d.**

# More Writing Fractions

**Directions:** Write a fraction for each picture.

1. 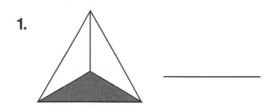 _____

2. 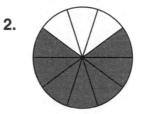 _____

3. 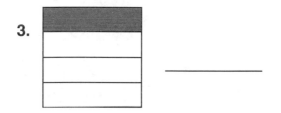 _____

4.  _____

5. 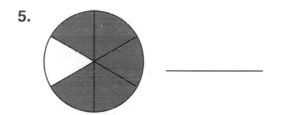 _____

6. 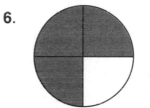 _____

7.  _____

8.  _____

# Fraction Fish

**Directions:** Color some fish in each bowl. Then write a fraction for the amount of fish you colored. For example, if you color 3 fish in the first bowl, you will write the fractional part $\frac{3}{5}$.

**1.**

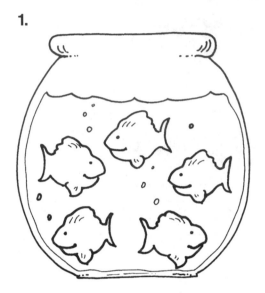

**2.**

**3.**

**4.**

# Beginning Fractions

**Directions:** Look at the chart. Complete the sentences.

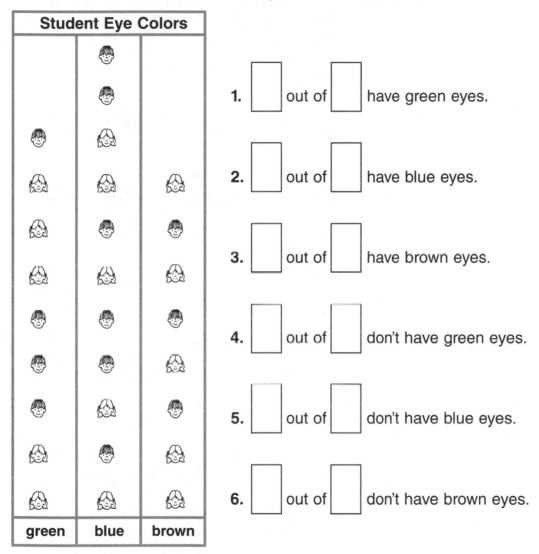

1. ☐ out of ☐ have green eyes.

2. ☐ out of ☐ have blue eyes.

3. ☐ out of ☐ have brown eyes.

4. ☐ out of ☐ don't have green eyes.

5. ☐ out of ☐ don't have blue eyes.

6. ☐ out of ☐ don't have brown eyes.

# Quarters

**Directions:** When something is divided into quarters, it is divided into fourths, just as four quarters make one dollar. Circle the pictures to divide into quarters, then color one quarter.

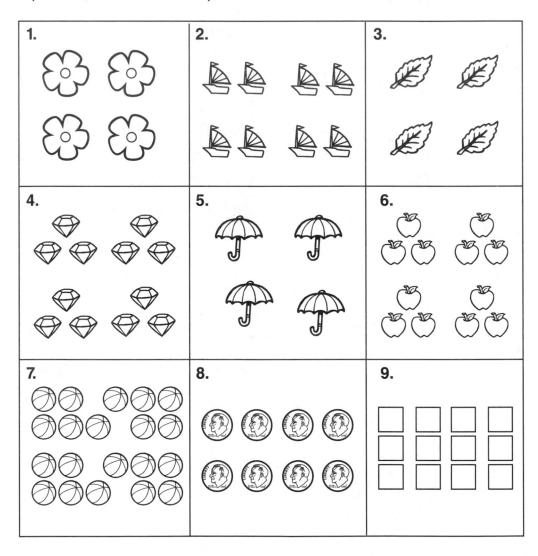

# Shading Parts

**Directions:** Shade the parts to match the fraction.

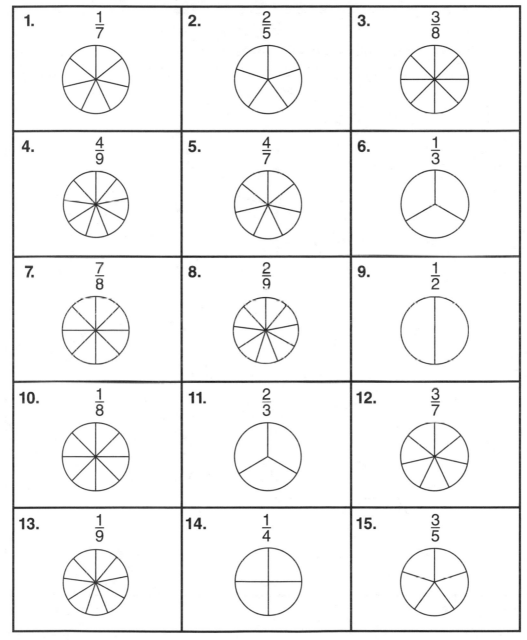

| 1. $\frac{1}{7}$ | 2. $\frac{2}{5}$ | 3. $\frac{3}{8}$ |
| 4. $\frac{4}{9}$ | 5. $\frac{4}{7}$ | 6. $\frac{1}{3}$ |
| 7. $\frac{7}{8}$ | 8. $\frac{2}{9}$ | 9. $\frac{1}{2}$ |
| 10. $\frac{1}{8}$ | 11. $\frac{2}{3}$ | 12. $\frac{3}{7}$ |
| 13. $\frac{1}{9}$ | 14. $\frac{1}{4}$ | 15. $\frac{3}{5}$ |

# What's the Fraction?

**Directions:** Identify each fraction. Use the key to color the puzzle.

| Key |
| --- |
| **halves = red**    **thirds = blue**    **quarters = yellow**    **fifths = green** |

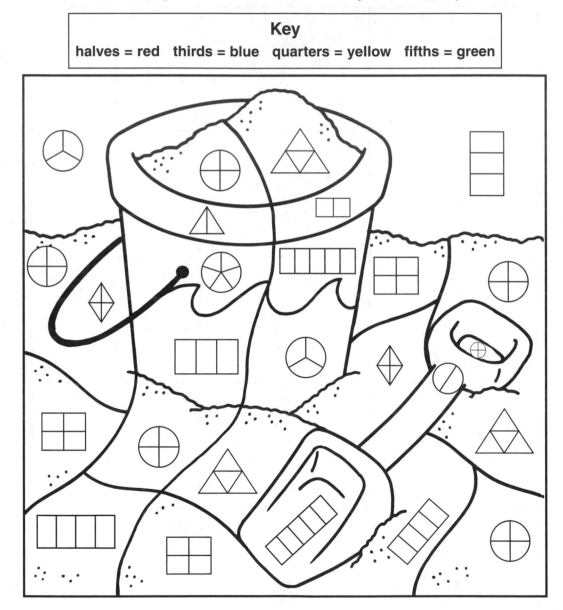

30

# Ordering Fractions

**Directions:** Shade the parts to show each fraction.

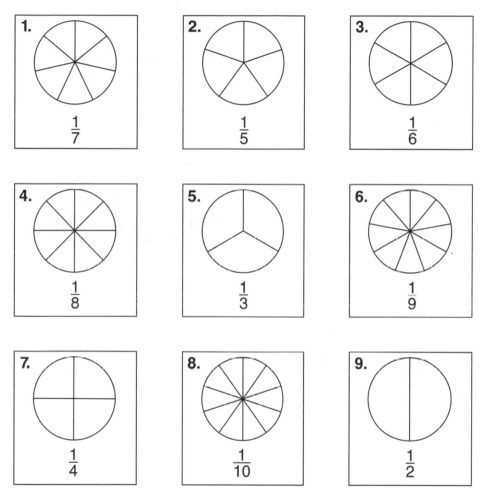

**Directions:** Write these fractions in order from largest to smallest.

_____, _____, _____, _____, _____, _____, _____, _____, _____

# Part of a Whole

**Directions:** Look at the shape. What fraction of the rectangle is shaded? Circle the correct answer.

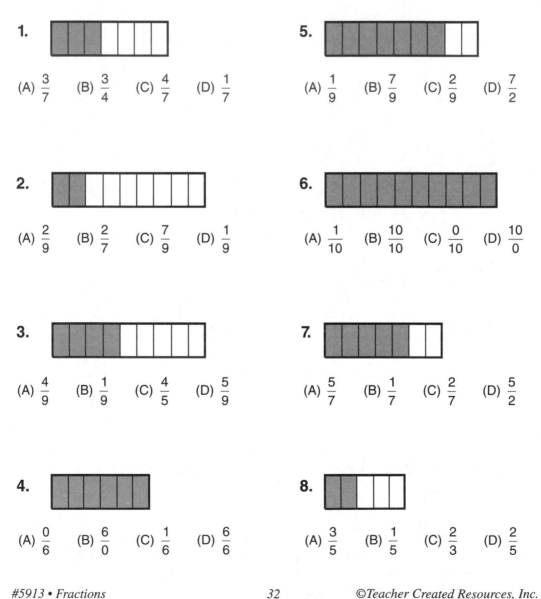

1.

(A) $\frac{3}{7}$   (B) $\frac{3}{4}$   (C) $\frac{4}{7}$   (D) $\frac{1}{7}$

5.

(A) $\frac{1}{9}$   (B) $\frac{7}{9}$   (C) $\frac{2}{9}$   (D) $\frac{7}{2}$

2.

(A) $\frac{2}{9}$   (B) $\frac{2}{7}$   (C) $\frac{7}{9}$   (D) $\frac{1}{9}$

6.

(A) $\frac{1}{10}$   (B) $\frac{10}{10}$   (C) $\frac{0}{10}$   (D) $\frac{10}{0}$

3.

(A) $\frac{4}{9}$   (B) $\frac{1}{9}$   (C) $\frac{4}{5}$   (D) $\frac{5}{9}$

7.

(A) $\frac{5}{7}$   (B) $\frac{1}{7}$   (C) $\frac{2}{7}$   (D) $\frac{5}{2}$

4.

(A) $\frac{0}{6}$   (B) $\frac{6}{0}$   (C) $\frac{1}{6}$   (D) $\frac{6}{6}$

8.

(A) $\frac{3}{5}$   (B) $\frac{1}{5}$   (C) $\frac{2}{3}$   (D) $\frac{2}{5}$

# Fraction Word Problems

**Directions:** Read each word problem. Circle your answer.

1. Darin **h**as 5 black marbles and 3 white marbles. From the total of black and white marbles, which fraction below shows the number of black marbles Darin has? (Circle the correct letter.)

**A.** $\frac{3}{3}$  **C.** $\frac{3}{8}$

**B.** $\frac{8}{3}$  **D.** $\frac{5}{8}$

2. Sam is counting the number of colored stickers he has. He found that $\frac{4}{5}$ of his stickers are black. Which answer below correctly represents Sam's stickers? (Circle the correct letter.)

**A.**   **C.**

**B.**   **D.**

3. Maci owns many shirts. More than $\frac{4}{8}$ of the shirts she owns have stripes. Which group could represent the shirts Maci owns? (Circle the correct letter.)

**A.**
**B.**
**C.**
**D.**

4. Jackie has a page of stickers. More than $\frac{6}{9}$ of the stickers are black. Which group could represent the page of stickers Jackie has? (Circle the correct letter.)

**A.**   **B.**   **C.**   **D.**

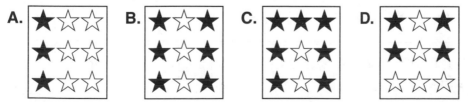

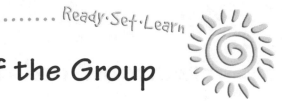
Ready·Set·Learn

# A Part of the Group

**Directions:** Look at each group and write a fraction for the answer.

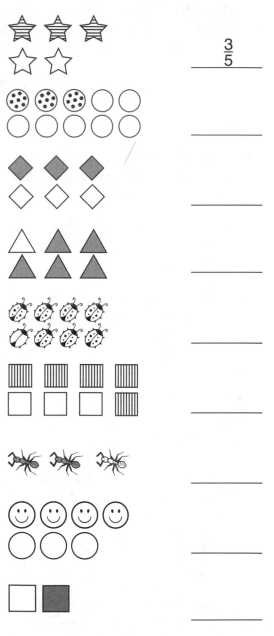

**Example:** What fraction of the stars have stripes?

$\frac{3}{5}$

1. What fraction of the circles have polka dots?

_____

2. What fraction of the diamonds are shaded?

_____

3. What fraction of the triangles are shaded?

_____

4. What fraction of the ladybugs have dots?

_____

5. What fraction of the squares have stripes?

_____

6. What fraction of the ants are shaded?

_____

7. What fraction of the circles have smiley faces?

_____

8. What fraction of the squares are shaded?

_____

# Fractions Riddle

**Directions:** On top of each circle is a letter. Find the fraction below that represents the circle. Write the letter on the line that shows the correct fraction.

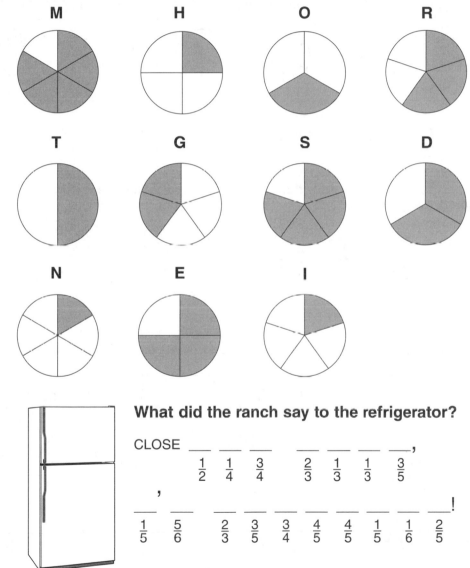

M   H   O   R

T   G   S   D

N   E   I

**What did the ranch say to the refrigerator?**

CLOSE ___ ___ ___   ___ ___ ___ ___,
$\frac{1}{2}$ $\frac{1}{4}$ $\frac{3}{4}$  $\frac{2}{3}$ $\frac{1}{3}$ $\frac{1}{3}$ $\frac{3}{5}$

, ___ ___   ___ ___ ___ ___ ___ ___ ___!
$\frac{1}{5}$ $\frac{5}{6}$  $\frac{2}{3}$ $\frac{3}{5}$ $\frac{3}{4}$ $\frac{4}{5}$ $\frac{4}{5}$ $\frac{1}{5}$ $\frac{1}{6}$ $\frac{2}{5}$

# Math Practice: Fractions

**Directions:** Read and follow each set of directions.

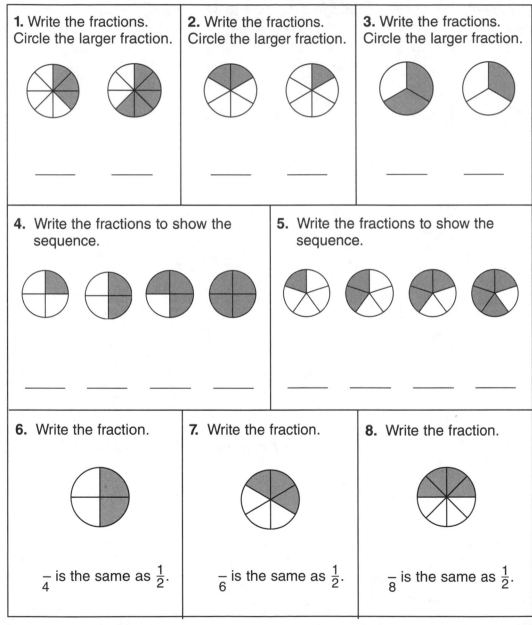

1. Write the fractions. Circle the larger fraction.

_____  _____

2. Write the fractions. Circle the larger fraction.

_____  _____

3. Write the fractions. Circle the larger fraction.

_____  _____

4. Write the fractions to show the sequence.

_____  _____  _____  _____

5. Write the fractions to show the sequence.

_____  _____  _____  _____

6. Write the fraction.

$\frac{}{4}$ is the same as $\frac{1}{2}$.

7. Write the fraction.

$\frac{}{6}$ is the same as $\frac{1}{2}$.

8. Write the fraction.

$\frac{}{8}$ is the same as $\frac{1}{2}$.

# Naming Fractions

**Directions:** Complete the fraction table below. Part of the table has already been filled in for you.

|  | ⬤ | ⬤ | ⬤ | ⬤ | ⬤ | ⬤ |
|---|---|---|---|---|---|---|
| **1.** How many parts does each circle have? |  |  | 3 |  | 5 | 6 |
| **2.** Using words, how much is each part of the shape? | one whole |  |  | one-fourth |  |  |
| **3.** What is the fraction for each part? |  | $\frac{1}{2}$ |  |  |  |  |

# Finding Equal Sets

**Directions:** How many equal sets can be made?  Circle the equal sets. Write the fraction for one set out of all of the sets.

| | |
|---|---|
| **Example:** Circle sets of 2. | **1.** Circle sets of 4. |
| _____7_____ equal sets can be made.<br><br>The fraction is _____$\frac{1}{7}$_____ . | _____ equal sets can be made.<br><br>The fraction is _____ . |
| **2.** Circle sets of 6. | **3.** Circle sets of 3. |
| _____ equal sets can be made.<br><br>The fraction is _____ . | _____ equal sets can be made.<br><br>The fraction is _____ . |
| **4.** Circle sets of 7. | **5.** Circle sets of 5. |
| _____ equal sets can be made.<br><br>The fraction is _____ . | _____ equal sets can be made.<br><br>The fraction is _____ . |

# Fractions of a Set (Thirds)

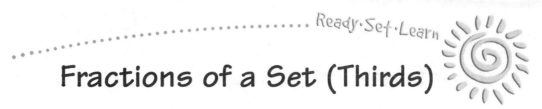

**Directions:** Circle one-third of the items in each set below, and then complete the math sentences. Write the fraction for each set of items on the last line. The first one has already been done for you.

**1.** There are ____9____ ____bones____. One-third of ____9____ is ____3____.

The fraction is ____$\frac{3}{9}$____.

**2.** There are _____ _____. One-third of _____ is _____.

The fraction is ____ _____.

**3.** There are _____ _____. One-third of _____ is _____.

The fraction is _____.

**4.** There are _____ _____. One-third of _____ is _____.

The fraction is _____.

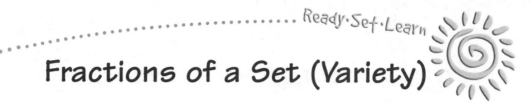

# Fractions of a Set (Variety)

**Directions:** Find the fraction set for each group below by circling the correct number of items. Check your answer by adding. The first one has already been done for you. Remember to show your work.

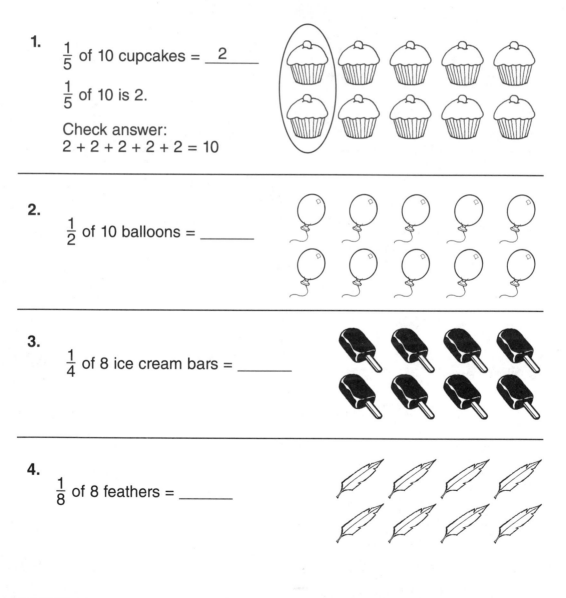

1.

$\frac{1}{5}$ of 10 cupcakes = ___2___

$\frac{1}{5}$ of 10 is 2.

Check answer:
2 + 2 + 2 + 2 + 2 = 10

2.

$\frac{1}{2}$ of 10 balloons = _____

3.

$\frac{1}{4}$ of 8 ice cream bars = _____

4.

$\frac{1}{8}$ of 8 feathers = _____

# Finding Part of a Whole

**Directions:** Circle the fractional amount. Complete the sentence.

**1.** $\frac{1}{3}$

$\frac{1}{3}$ of 9 frogs is _____ frogs.

**2.** $\frac{3}{5}$

$\frac{3}{5}$ of 10 rabbits is _____ rabbits.

**3.** $\frac{3}{4}$

$\frac{3}{4}$ of 8 pigs is _____ pigs.

**4.** $\frac{2}{3}$

$\frac{2}{3}$ of 9 tigers is _____ tigers.

**5.** $\frac{3}{8}$

$\frac{3}{8}$ of 8 dogs is _____ dogs.

**6.** $\frac{1}{2}$

$\frac{1}{2}$ of 10 owls is _____ owls.

# Comparing Fractions

**Directions:** Compare the two fractions using the ">" (greater than) and "<" (less than) symbols. Then write the math sentence. The first one has already been done for you.

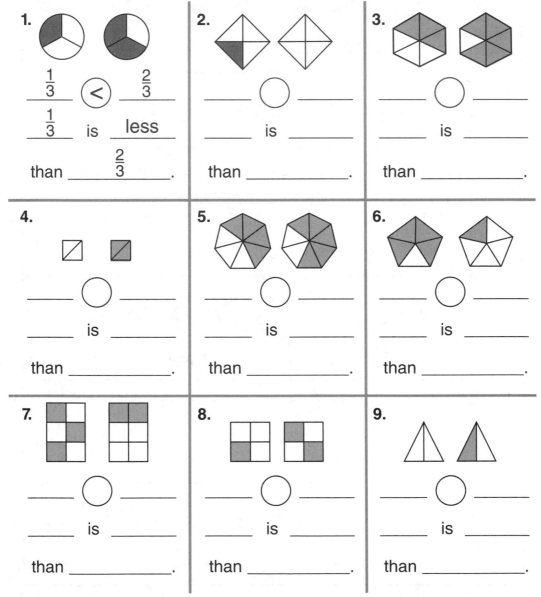

**1.**

$$\frac{1}{3} < \frac{2}{3}$$

$\frac{1}{3}$ is __less__

than ____$\frac{2}{3}$____ .

**2.**

____ ◯ ____

____ is ____

than _____ .

**3.**

____ ◯ ____

____ is ____

than _____ .

**4.**

____ ◯ ____

____ is ____

than _____ .

**5.**

____ ◯ ____

____ is ____

than _____ .

**6.**

____ ◯ ____

____ is ____

than _____ .

**7.**

____ ◯ ____

____ is ____

than _____ .

**8.**

____ ◯ ____

____ is ____

than _____ .

**9.**

____ ◯ ____

____ is ____

than _____ .

42

# Finding the
# Largest Fraction

**Directions:** Name each fraction. Then circle the largest fraction in each group.

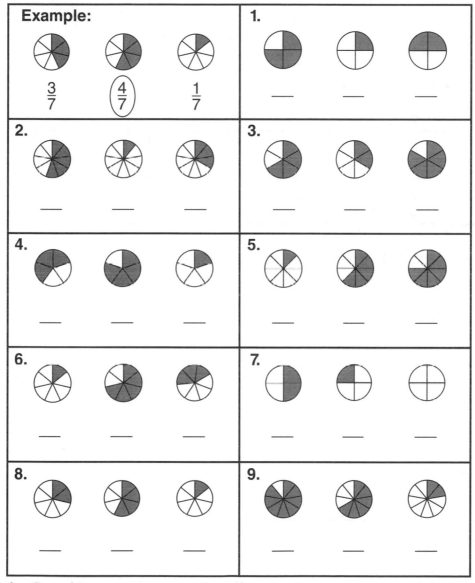

# Comparing Fractions

**Directions:** When comparing fractions with the same denominator, look at the numerator. The larger the numerator, the larger the fraction. Look at the two fractions and circle the larger fraction.

| | | | | | | | | |
|---|---|---|---|---|---|---|---|---|
| **1.** | $\frac{3}{4}$ $\frac{1}{4}$ | **2.** | $\frac{2}{9}$ $\frac{4}{9}$ | **3.** | $\frac{4}{5}$ $\frac{2}{5}$ |
| **4.** | $\frac{3}{7}$ $\frac{4}{7}$ | **5.** | $\frac{9}{10}$ $\frac{4}{10}$ | **6.** | $\frac{7}{8}$ $\frac{6}{8}$ |
| **7.** | $\frac{1}{6}$ $\frac{5}{6}$ | **8.** | $\frac{2}{7}$ $\frac{1}{7}$ | **9.** | $\frac{3}{10}$ $\frac{6}{10}$ |
| **10.** | $\frac{6}{9}$ $\frac{1}{9}$ | **11.** | $\frac{1}{5}$ $\frac{3}{5}$ | **12.** | $\frac{1}{3}$ $\frac{2}{3}$ |
| **13.** | $\frac{3}{8}$ $\frac{2}{8}$ | **14.** | $\frac{2}{6}$ $\frac{3}{6}$ | **15.** | $\frac{5}{7}$ $\frac{4}{7}$ |

**Directions:** Write the fractions in order, from smallest to largest.

16. $\frac{5}{8}, \frac{1}{8}, \frac{3}{8}$ _____, _____, _____

17. $\frac{7}{9}, \frac{6}{9}, \frac{8}{9}$ _____, _____, _____

18. $\frac{4}{7}, \frac{5}{7}, \frac{1}{7}$ _____, _____, _____

19. $\frac{3}{6}, \frac{5}{6}, \frac{2}{6}$ _____, _____, _____

20. $\frac{3}{4}, \frac{2}{4}, \frac{1}{4}$ _____, _____, _____

# Fraction
# Number Lines

**Directions:** A fraction is a part of a whole item or amount. Complete each fraction number line. Then write the fraction the arrow is pointing to on the line.

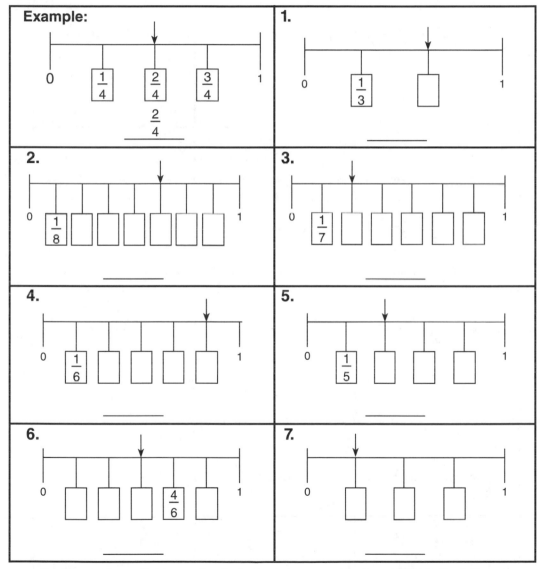

# Identifying Fractions
# Using a Number Line

**Directions:** Identify the fraction. Circle the answer.

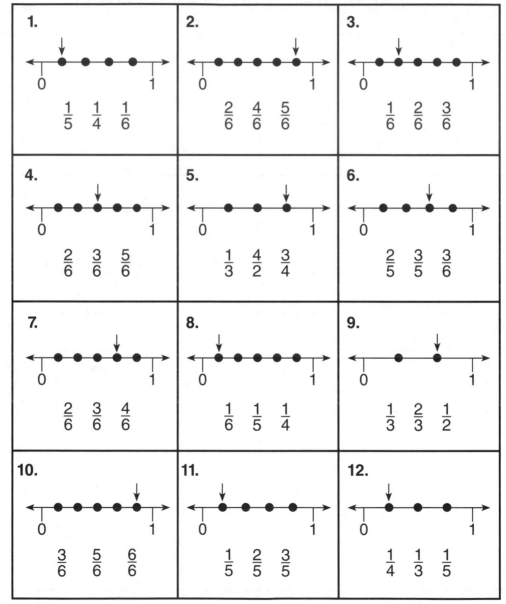

1.

$\frac{1}{5}$  $\frac{1}{4}$  $\frac{1}{6}$

2.

$\frac{2}{6}$  $\frac{4}{6}$  $\frac{5}{6}$

3.

$\frac{1}{6}$  $\frac{2}{6}$  $\frac{3}{6}$

4.

$\frac{2}{6}$  $\frac{3}{6}$  $\frac{5}{6}$

5.

$\frac{1}{3}$  $\frac{4}{2}$  $\frac{3}{4}$

6.

$\frac{2}{5}$  $\frac{3}{5}$  $\frac{3}{6}$

7.

$\frac{2}{6}$  $\frac{3}{6}$  $\frac{4}{6}$

8.

$\frac{1}{6}$  $\frac{1}{5}$  $\frac{1}{4}$

9.

$\frac{1}{3}$  $\frac{2}{3}$  $\frac{1}{2}$

10.

$\frac{3}{6}$  $\frac{5}{6}$  $\frac{6}{6}$

11.

$\frac{1}{5}$  $\frac{2}{5}$  $\frac{3}{5}$

12.

$\frac{1}{4}$  $\frac{1}{3}$  $\frac{1}{5}$

46

# Finding Equivalent Fractions

**Directions:** Color in $\frac{1}{2}$ of the first shape in each pair. On the second shape, color in the same amount of area. Write the equivalent fraction on the line. The first one has been done for you.

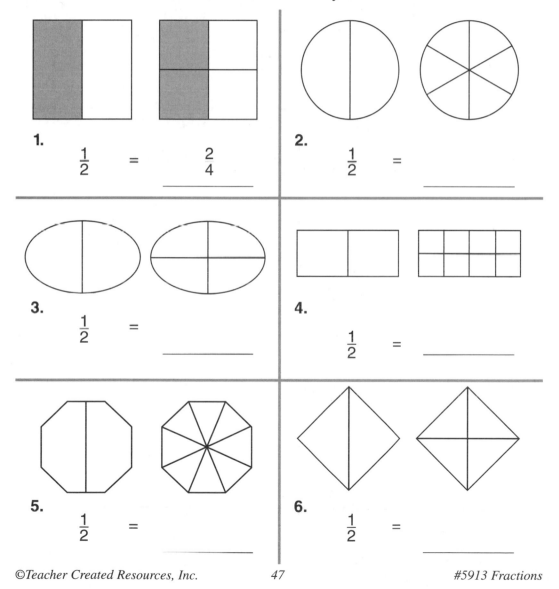

1. $\frac{1}{2}$ = $\frac{2}{4}$

2. $\frac{1}{2}$ = _____

3. $\frac{1}{2}$ = _____

4. $\frac{1}{2}$ = _____

5. $\frac{1}{2}$ = _____

6. $\frac{1}{2}$ = _____

# Adding Fractions with Like Denominators

**Directions:** If the denominators are the same, just add the numerators together. (The denominator stays the same.) Add the fractions. The first two are done for you.

1. $\frac{1}{2} + \frac{1}{2} = \frac{2}{2}$

2. $\frac{1}{3} + \frac{1}{3} = \frac{2}{3}$

3. $\frac{3}{4} + \frac{1}{4} = \underline{\hspace{1cm}}$

4. $\frac{2}{5} + \frac{2}{5} = \underline{\hspace{1cm}}$

5. $\frac{2}{6} + \frac{2}{6} = \underline{\hspace{1cm}}$

6. $\frac{4}{5} + \frac{1}{5} = \underline{\hspace{1cm}}$

7. $\frac{2}{5} + \frac{1}{5} = \underline{\hspace{1cm}}$

8. $\frac{3}{5} + \frac{1}{5} = \underline{\hspace{1cm}}$

9. $\frac{1}{6} + \frac{4}{6} = \underline{\hspace{1cm}}$

10. $\frac{2}{4} + \frac{2}{4} = \underline{\hspace{1cm}}$

11. $\frac{3}{6} + \frac{2}{6} = \underline{\hspace{1cm}}$

12. $\frac{1}{4} + \frac{1}{4} = \underline{\hspace{1cm}}$

13. $\frac{3}{6} + \frac{3}{6} = \underline{\hspace{1cm}}$

14. $\frac{2}{3} + \frac{1}{3} = \underline{\hspace{1cm}}$

15. $\frac{1}{6} + \frac{1}{6} = \underline{\hspace{1cm}}$

# Adding Fractions

**Directions:** Follow the directions given in each box.

| | | |
|---|---|---|
| **1.** Add. $$\frac{1}{3} + \frac{1}{3} =$$ | **2.** Add. $$\frac{4}{8} + \frac{3}{8} =$$ | **3.** Add. $$\frac{1}{6} + \frac{1}{6} =$$ |

**4.** Write the problem, and then solve it.

Clarice ate $\frac{1}{4}$ of a pumpkin pie, and Clarence ate $\frac{2}{4}$ of a pumpkin pie. How much pie did they eat in all?

They ate _____ of a pie in all.

**5.** Write the problem, and then solve it.

Pamela and Harrison each ate $\frac{2}{5}$ of a candy bar. How much of the candy bar did they eat in all?

They ate _____ of a candy bar.

| | | |
|---|---|---|
| **6.** Add. $$\frac{1}{8} + \frac{5}{8} =$$ | **7.** Add. $$\frac{2}{6} + \frac{3}{6} =$$ | **8.** Add. $$\frac{4}{7} + \frac{1}{7} =$$ |

# Subtracting Fractions
# With Like Denominators

**Directions:** If the denominators are the same, just subtract the numerators. (The denominator stays the same.) Subtract the fractions and circle the correct answer.

1. $\dfrac{5}{7} - \dfrac{1}{7} =$      (A) 4      (B) $\dfrac{4}{7}$      (C) $\dfrac{6}{7}$      (D) $\dfrac{5}{7}$

2. $\dfrac{3}{17} - \dfrac{2}{17} =$      (A) 1      (B) $\dfrac{2}{17}$      (C) $\dfrac{1}{17}$      (D) $\dfrac{5}{17}$

3. $\dfrac{12}{13} - \dfrac{11}{13} =$      (A) $\dfrac{1}{13}$      (B) $\dfrac{2}{13}$      (C) $\dfrac{23}{13}$      (D) 1

4. $\dfrac{5}{13} - \dfrac{2}{13} =$      (A) 3      (B) $\dfrac{4}{13}$      (C) $\dfrac{7}{13}$      (D) $\dfrac{3}{13}$

5. $\dfrac{8}{13} - \dfrac{7}{13} =$      (A) $\dfrac{2}{13}$      (B) $\dfrac{15}{13}$      (C) $\dfrac{1}{13}$      (D) 1

6. $\dfrac{6}{11} - \dfrac{1}{11} =$      (A) $\dfrac{7}{11}$      (B) 5      (C) $\dfrac{6}{11}$      (D) $\dfrac{5}{11}$

# Subtracting Fractions

**Directions:** Follow the directions given in each box.

---

**1.** Subtract.

$$\frac{6}{7} - \frac{3}{7} = \underline{\quad}$$

**2.** Subtract.

$$\frac{3}{8} - \frac{1}{8} = \underline{\quad}$$

**3.** Subtract.

$$\frac{2}{4} - \frac{1}{4} = \underline{\quad}$$

---

**4.** Write the problem, and then solve it.

The sugar bowl holds $\frac{3}{4}$ of a cup. Marnie used $\frac{1}{4}$ of a cup of sugar. How much sugar is left in the bowl?

There is _____ cup of sugar left.

**5.** Write the problem, and then solve it.

The container held $\frac{5}{6}$ of a cup of car wax. Harvey used $\frac{3}{6}$ of a cup to wax the car. How much wax is left?

There is _____ cup of wax left.

---

**6.** Subtract.

$$\frac{9}{10} - \frac{8}{10} = \underline{\quad}$$

**7.** Subtract.

$$\frac{8}{9} - \frac{4}{9} = \underline{\quad}$$

**8.** Subtract.

$$\frac{6}{7} - \frac{3}{7} = \underline{\quad}$$

---

# Adding and Subtracting Fractions

**Directions:** When the denominators of fractions are the same, those fractions can be added or subtracted easily.

$$\frac{1}{4} + \frac{2}{4} = \frac{3}{4} \qquad \text{and} \qquad \frac{3}{4} - \frac{1}{4} = \frac{2}{4}$$

Notice that the bottom number (the denominator) stays the same—only the top number (the numerator) changes.

**Directions:** Add the following fractions.

1. $\frac{2}{5} + \frac{3}{5} =$ _____

2. $\frac{1}{8} + \frac{4}{8} =$ _____

3. $\frac{1}{3} + \frac{1}{3} =$ _____

4. $\frac{2}{6} + \frac{3}{6} =$ _____

5. $\frac{1}{4} + \frac{3}{4} =$ _____

6. $\frac{4}{10} + \frac{3}{10} =$ _____

**Directions:** Subtract the following fractions.

7. $\frac{4}{8} - \frac{1}{8} =$ _____

8. $\frac{5}{6} - \frac{2}{6} =$ _____

9. $\frac{7}{10} - \frac{3}{10} =$ _____

10. $\frac{3}{4} - \frac{2}{4} =$ _____

11. $\frac{3}{3} - \frac{2}{3} =$ _____

12. $\frac{8}{9} - \frac{6}{9} =$ _____

**Directions:** Solve the problem and draw a picture to represent the answer.

13. $\frac{2}{3} + \frac{1}{3} =$ _____

# Adding and Subtracting Fractions with Like Denominators

**Directions:** Add or subtract.

1. $\dfrac{3}{4} - \dfrac{2}{4} =$ _____

2. $\dfrac{2}{5} + \dfrac{1}{5} =$ _____

3. $\dfrac{3}{6} + \dfrac{2}{6} =$ _____

4. $\dfrac{2}{9} + \dfrac{6}{9} =$ _____

5. $\dfrac{5}{7} - \dfrac{3}{7} =$ _____

6. $\dfrac{8}{9} - \dfrac{4}{9} =$ _____

7. $\dfrac{2}{4} + \dfrac{1}{4} =$ _____

8. $\dfrac{2}{9} + \dfrac{3}{9} =$ _____

9. $\dfrac{2}{3} - \dfrac{1}{3} =$ _____

10. $\dfrac{5}{8} - \dfrac{1}{8} =$ _____

11. $\dfrac{3}{9} - \dfrac{1}{9} =$ _____

12. $\dfrac{4}{8} - \dfrac{2}{8} =$ _____

13. $\dfrac{1}{6} + \dfrac{4}{6} =$ _____

14. $\dfrac{1}{7} + \dfrac{3}{7} =$ _____

15. $\dfrac{5}{8} + \dfrac{2}{8} =$ _____

**Directions:** Read and solve each word problem.

| | |
|---|---|
| **16.** The recipe calls for $\frac{1}{4}$ of a cup of brown sugar and $\frac{1}{4}$ of a cup of white sugar. How much sugar is needed in all? <br><br> _____ of a cup of sugar | **17.** In a glass, Dave mixed $\frac{1}{5}$ of a cup of chocolate milk with $\frac{2}{5}$ of a cup of white milk. How much liquid is in the glass? <br><br> _____ of a cup of liquid |
| **18.** Sue had $\frac{2}{3}$ of a cup of jellybeans. She ate $\frac{1}{3}$ of a cup of jellybeans. How much did she have left? <br><br> _____ of a cup | **19.** To make the dressing, pour $\frac{1}{5}$ of a cup of vinegar and $\frac{3}{5}$ of a cup of oil into a bowl. How much dressing is made? <br><br> _____ of a cup of dressing |

# Equal Parts

**Directions:** Read each word problem. Divide a shape or circle a fraction to show the answer.

| | |
|---|---|
| **1.** Jenni and Drew want to share a candy bar. Draw a line to show how Jenni and Drew will get equal amounts of the candy bar. | **4.** George, Angie, and Nicky want to equally share a small, round pizza. Circle the fraction that shows what part each one will get. |
| **2.** Kyle and Terri have a bag of jellybeans. How much of the bag will each get if they want the same amount of jellybeans? | **5.** Sophia and Maria want to share a sandwich. Draw a line on the sandwich to show how they will get equal parts of the sandwich. |
| **3.** Mrs. Long and her three children want to share a pizza. Divide the pizza into equal parts so that they all get the same amount. | **6.** Judy and her mom and dad want to share a chocolate bar. Draw lines to show how Judy, her mom, and her dad will get equal parts of the chocolate bar. |

$\frac{1}{2}$    $\frac{1}{4}$    $\frac{1}{3}$

$\frac{1}{2}$    $\frac{1}{4}$    $\frac{1}{3}$

# Math Practice: Fractions

**Directions:** Follow the directions given in each box.

**1.** How many turtles are in the fraction?

$\frac{1}{2}$ of 6 = _____

**2.** How many frogs are in the fraction?

$\frac{1}{2}$ of 4 = _____

**3.** How many rabbits are in the fraction?

$\frac{1}{2}$ of 2 = _____

**4.** Use division to find the number in a fraction.

$\frac{1}{3}$ of 9 = _____

9 ÷ 3 = _____

**5.** Use division to find the number in a fraction.

$\frac{1}{4}$ of 8 = _____

8 ÷ 4 = _____

**6.** Shade the shape to show the equivalent fraction. Write the fraction.

$\frac{1}{2}$ =

_____

**7.** Shade the shape to show the equivalent fraction. Write the fraction.

$\frac{2}{3}$ =

_____

**8.** Shade the shape to show the equivalent fraction. Write the fraction.

$\frac{3}{4}$ =

_____

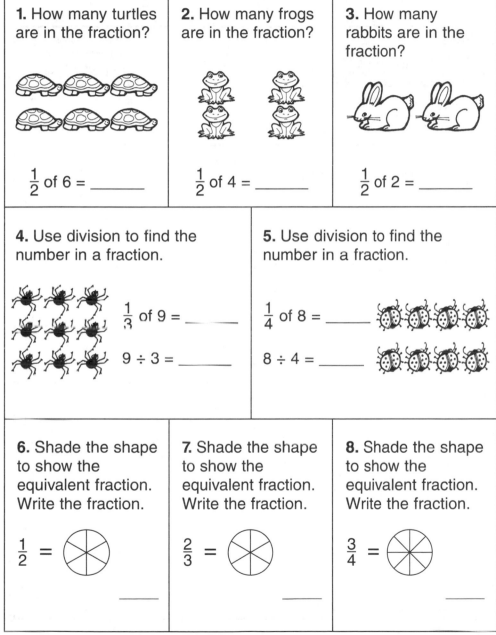

# Comparing Fractions

**Directions:** Shade to show the correct fraction. Then circle the larger fraction.

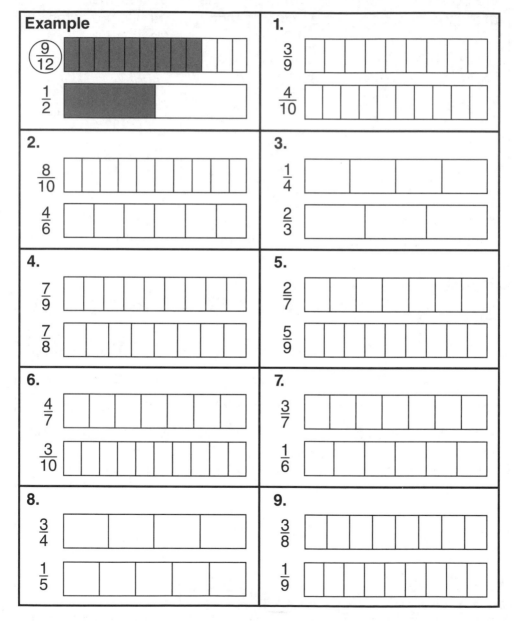

**Example**
$\dfrac{9}{12}$
$\dfrac{1}{2}$

**1.**
$\dfrac{3}{9}$
$\dfrac{4}{10}$

**2.**
$\dfrac{8}{10}$
$\dfrac{4}{6}$

**3.**
$\dfrac{1}{4}$
$\dfrac{2}{3}$

**4.**
$\dfrac{7}{9}$
$\dfrac{7}{8}$

**5.**
$\dfrac{2}{7}$
$\dfrac{5}{9}$

**6.**
$\dfrac{4}{7}$
$\dfrac{3}{10}$

**7.**
$\dfrac{3}{7}$
$\dfrac{1}{6}$

**8.**
$\dfrac{3}{4}$
$\dfrac{1}{5}$

**9.**
$\dfrac{3}{8}$
$\dfrac{1}{9}$

# Finding Equal Sets

**Directions:** How many equal sets can be made?  Circle equal sets.
Write the fraction for one set out of all of the sets.

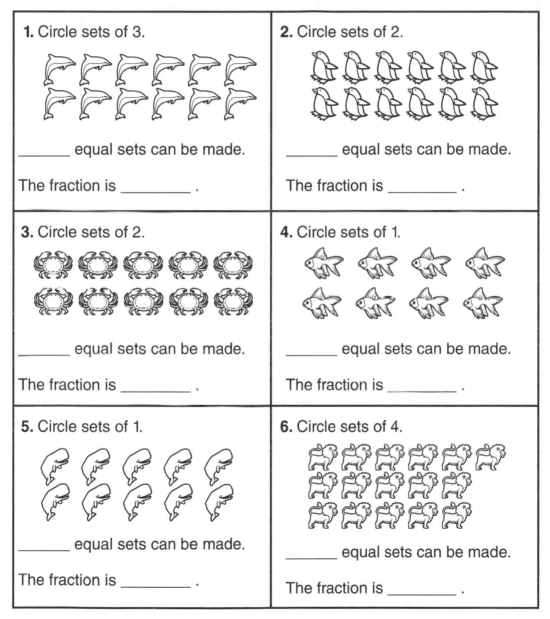

**1.** Circle sets of 3.

_____ equal sets can be made.

The fraction is _____ .

**2.** Circle sets of 2.

_____ equal sets can be made.

The fraction is _____ .

**3.** Circle sets of 2.

_____ equal sets can be made.

The fraction is _____ .

**4.** Circle sets of 1.

_____ equal sets can be made.

The fraction is _____ .

**5.** Circle sets of 1.

_____ equal sets can be made.

The fraction is _____ .

**6.** Circle sets of 4.

_____ equal sets can be made.

The fraction is _____ .

# Representing Money
# as Fractions

**Directions:** Write each amount of money as a fraction. The first one has already been done for you.

**1.**

9¢  $\dfrac{9}{100}$

**2.**

44¢ ———

**3.**

98¢ ———

**4.**

65¢ ———

**5.**

39¢ ———

**6.**

27¢ ———

**7.**

$0.73 ———

**8.**

$0.88 ———

**9.**

$0.23 ———

**10.**

$0.15 ———

**11.**

$0.50 ———

**12.**

$0.11 ———

**Directions:** Use the > (greater than), < (less than), or = (equal to) symbols to compare the numbers. The first one has already been done for you.

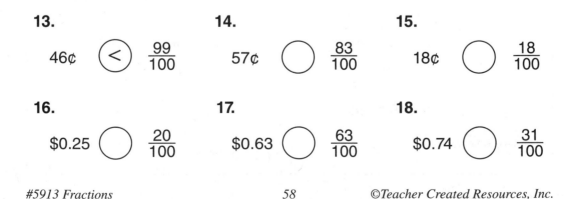

**13.**

46¢  $<$  $\dfrac{99}{100}$

**14.**

57¢  ◯  $\dfrac{83}{100}$

**15.**

18¢  ◯  $\dfrac{18}{100}$

**16.**

$0.25  ◯  $\dfrac{20}{100}$

**17.**

$0.63  ◯  $\dfrac{63}{100}$

**18.**

$0.74  ◯  $\dfrac{31}{100}$

# Comparing Fractions

**Directions:** Shade to show the correct fraction. Then use the symbols > (greater than) or < (less than) to compare the two fractions.

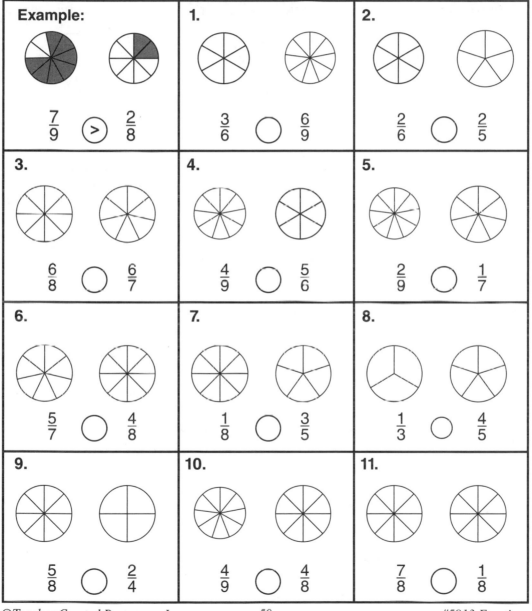

**Example:**

$\frac{7}{9}$ ⊙(>) $\frac{2}{8}$

**1.**

$\frac{3}{6}$ ◯ $\frac{6}{9}$

**2.**

$\frac{2}{6}$ ◯ $\frac{2}{5}$

**3.**

$\frac{6}{8}$ ◯ $\frac{6}{7}$

**4.**

$\frac{4}{9}$ ◯ $\frac{5}{6}$

**5.**

$\frac{2}{9}$ ◯ $\frac{1}{7}$

**6.**

$\frac{5}{7}$ ◯ $\frac{4}{8}$

**7.**

$\frac{1}{8}$ ◯ $\frac{3}{5}$

**8.**

$\frac{1}{3}$ ◯ $\frac{4}{5}$

**9.**

$\frac{5}{8}$ ◯ $\frac{2}{4}$

**10.**

$\frac{4}{9}$ ◯ $\frac{4}{8}$

**11.**

$\frac{7}{8}$ ◯ $\frac{1}{8}$

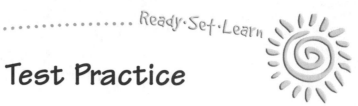

# Test Practice

**Directions:** Circle the correct answer.

| | | |
|---|---|---|
| **1.** What's the fraction for the shaded part? <br><br> (A) $\frac{1}{4}$ (B) $\frac{3}{4}$ (C) $\frac{2}{4}$ | **2.** What's the fraction for the shaded part? <br><br> (A) $\frac{3}{5}$ (B) $\frac{2}{5}$ (C) $\frac{2}{3}$ | **3.** What's the fraction for the shaded part? <br><br> (A) $\frac{7}{8}$ (B) $\frac{3}{8}$ (C) $\frac{5}{8}$ |
| **4.** Name the largest fraction. <br><br> (A) $\frac{3}{7}$ (B) $\frac{2}{7}$ (C) $\frac{4}{7}$ | **5.** Name the largest fraction. <br><br> (A) $\frac{2}{6}$ (B) $\frac{1}{6}$ (C) $\frac{4}{6}$ | **6.** Name the smallest fraction. <br><br> (A) $\frac{5}{9}$ (B) $\frac{3}{9}$ (C) $\frac{1}{9}$ |
| **7.** Which fraction names a whole item or amount? <br><br> (A) $\frac{1}{8}$ (B) $\frac{8}{8}$ (C) $\frac{3}{8}$ | **8.** Add the fractions. <br><br> $\frac{1}{4} + \frac{2}{4} =$ <br><br> (A) $\frac{3}{4}$ (B) $\frac{2}{16}$ (C) $\frac{3}{8}$ | **9.** Add the fractions. <br><br> $\frac{3}{5} + \frac{1}{5} =$ <br><br> (A) $\frac{4}{10}$ (B) $\frac{4}{5}$ (C) $\frac{4}{25}$ |
| **10.** Subtract the fractions. <br><br> $\frac{5}{8} - \frac{3}{8} =$ <br><br> (A) $\frac{2}{0}$ (B) $\frac{8}{8}$ (C) $\frac{2}{8}$ | **11.** Subtract the fractions. <br><br> $\frac{7}{9} - \frac{6}{9} =$ <br><br> (A) $\frac{9}{1}$ (B) $\frac{13}{9}$ (C) $\frac{1}{9}$ | **12.** Subtract the fractions. <br><br> $\frac{6}{7} - \frac{4}{7} =$ <br><br> (A) $\frac{2}{7}$ (B) $\frac{10}{7}$ (C) $\frac{2}{0}$ |

# Answer Key

**Page 4**
1. 2    7. 5
2. 5    8. 8
3. 4    9. 4
4. 3    10. 8
5. 6    11. 7
6. 2    12. 10

**Page 5**
1. 2    7. 1
2. 1    8. 2
3. 1    9. 1
4. 3    10. 4
5. 8    11. 1
6. 4    12. 2

**Page 6**
Check answers to see that the directions have been followed.

**Page 7**
1. no    7. yes
2. no    8. no
3. yes   9. no
4. no    10. no
5. no    11. yes
6. yes   12. no

**Page 8**
1. 2 shapes should be circled.
2. 1 shape should be circled.
3. 2 shapes should be circled.
4. 2 shapes should be circled.
5. 1 shape should be circled.

**Page 9**
1. 1    6. 1
2. 2    7. 3
3. 1    8. 2
4. 3    9. 3
5. 7

**Pages 10-11**
Check answers to see that the directions have been followed.

**Page 12**
1. 5    9. 4
2. 1    10. 4
3. 3    11. 7
4. 4    12. 7
5. 8    13. 4
6. 6    14. 2
7. 1    15. 1
8. 2    16. 2

**Page 13**
1. 1/3    7. 5/9
2. 4/6    8. 1/4
3. 2/5    9. 3/4
4. 0/4    10. 3/6
5. 1/2    11. 2/4
6. 1/2    12. 2/3

**Page 14**
1. b    3. d
2. c    4. a

**Page 15**
1. 1/2
2. 2/4
3. 4/7
4. <
5. >
6. 1 of 2 sections should be shaded
7. 5 of 6 sections should be shaded

8. 3 of 7 sections should be shaded
9. 2/3
10. 4/4

**Page 16**
1. 1/3
2. 1/6
3. 2/8
4. 1/4
5. 1/8
6. 3/4
7. 5/6
8. 2/5
9. 2/9
10. 4/8
11. 3/6
12. 4/5

**Page 17**
4. 3/8
5. 3/6
6. 3/4
7. 2/3
8. 1/6
9. ¼, 1/2
10. ½, 1/3

**Page 18**
1. 1/3
2. 2/4
3. 3/4
4. 2/3
5. 4/4
6. 3/3
7. 1/4
8. 2/5

**Page 19**
1. 2/3    4. 1/3
2. 1/4    5. 3/5
3. 1/2    6. 2/5

**Page 20**
1. 4/8    4. 1/2
2. 1/4    5. 3/8
3. 2/3    6. 1/3

**Page 21**
1. 1/2    6. 1/6
2. 1/7    7. 1/3
3. 1/9    8. 1/1
4. 5/10   9. 8
5. 3/9    10. 6

**Page 22**
Check answers to see that the directions have been followed.

**Page 23**
1. 1/5, one-fifth
2. 1/4, one-fourth
3. 3/8, three-eighths
4. 1/3, one-third
5. 7/8, seven-eighths
6. ¾, three-fourths
7. 1/6, one-sixth
8. 2/5, two-fifths
9. 2/3, two-thirds

**Page 24**
1. 2, 6; 1, 3; 4, 7
2. Check to see that the directions have been followed.
3. 1, 4; 2, 3; 6, 12
4. Check to see that the directions have been followed.

**Page 25**
1. 1/3
2. 7/10
3. 1/4
4. 2/6
5. 5/6
6. 3/4
7. 3/5
8. 1/2

**Page 26**
Check answers to see that the directions have been followed.

**Page 27**
1. 9 out of 28
2. 11 out of 28
3. 8 out of 28
4. 19 out of 28
5. 17 out of 28
6. 20 out of 28

**Pages 28–31**
Check answers to see that the directions have been followed.

**Page 32**
1. A    5. B
2. A    6. B
3. A    7. A
4. D    8. D

**Page 33**
1. D    3. C
2. C    4. C

**Page 34**
1. 3/10    5. 5/8
2. 3/6     6. 2/3
3. 5/6     7. 4/7
4. 7/8     8. 1/2

# Answer Key (cont.)

**Page 35**
Answer: Close the door, I'm dressing!

**Page 36**
1. 3/8, 5/8
2. 2/6, 1/6
3. 2/3, 1/3
4. ¼, 2/4, ¾, 4/4
5. 1/5, 2/5, 3/5, 4/5
6. 2
7. 3
8. 4

**Page 37**

| 1. How many parts does each circle have? | 1 | 2 | 3 | 4 | 5 | 6 |
|---|---|---|---|---|---|---|
| 2. Using words, how much is each part of the shape? | one whole | one half | one third | one-fourth | one fifth | one sixth |
| 3. What is the fraction for each part? | 1/1 | 1/2 | 1/3 | 1/4 | 1/5 | 1/6 |

**Page 38**
1. 3, 1/3
2. 2, 1/2
3. 3, 1/3
4. 2, 1/2
5. 2, 1/2

**Page 39**
1. 6 books, 6, 2, 2/6
2. 3 cones, 3, 1, 1/3
3. 12 apples, 12, 4, 4/12

**Page 40**
1. 2     3. 2
2. 5     4. 1

**Page 41**
1. 3     4. 6
2. 6     5. 3
3. 6     6. 5

**Page 42**
1. 1/3 < 2/3
2. ¼ > 0/4
3. 3/6 < 5/6
4. 0/2 < 2/2
5. 4/7< 5/7
6. 4/5 > 1/5
7. 3/6 > 2/6
8. ¼ < 2/4
9. 0/2 < 1/2

**Page 43**
1. ¾, ¼, 2/4
2. 5/9, 1/9, 3/9
3. 4/6, 2/6, 5/6
4. 3/5, 4/5, 1/5
5. 1/8, 5/8, 6/8
6. 1/7, 5/7, 3/7
7. 2/4, ¼, 0/4
8. 2/7, 4/7, 1/7
9. 8/9, 6/9, 2/9

**Page 44**
1. 3/4
2. 4/9
3. 4/5
4. 4/7
5. 9/10
6. 7/8
7. 5/6
8. 2/7
9. 6/10
10. 6/9
11. 3/5
12. 2/3
13. 3/8
14. 3/6
15. 5/7
16. 1/8, 3/8, 5/8
17. 6/9, 7/9, 8/9
18. 1/7, 4/7, 5/7
19. 2/6, 3/6, 5/6
20. ¼, 2/4, 3/4

**Page 45**
1. 2/3     5. 2/5
2. 5/8     6. 3/6
3. 2/7     7. 1/4
4. 5/6

**Page 46**
1. 1/5     7. 4/6
2. 5/6     8. 1/6
3. 2/6     9. 2/3
4. 3/6    10. 5/6
5. 3/4    11. 1/5
6. 3/5    12. 1/4

**Page 47**
1. 2/4     4. 4/8
2. 3/6     5. 4/8
3. 2/4     6. 2/4

**Page 48**
1. 2/2     9. 5/6
2. 2/3    10. 4/4
3. 4/4    11. 5/6
4. 4/5    12. 2/4
5. 4/6    13. 6/6
6. 5/5    14. 3/3
7. 3/5    15. 2/6
8. 4/5

**Page 49**
1. 2/3     5. 4/5
2. 7/8     6. 6/8
3. 2/6     7. 5/6
4. 3/4     8. 5/7

**Page 50**
1. B     4. D
2. C     5. C
3. A     6. D

**Page 51**
1. 3/7     5. 2/6
2. 2/8     6. 1/10
3. 1/4     7. 4/9
4. 2/4     8. 3/7

**Page 52**
1. 5/5
2. 5/8
3. 2/3

4. 5/6
5. 4/4
6. 7/10
7. 3/8
8. 3/6
9. 4/10
10. 1/4
11. 1/3
12. 2/9
13. 3/3

**Page 53**
1. 1/4     11. 2/9
2. 3/5     12. 2/8
3. 5/6     13. 5/6
4. 8/9     14. 4/7
5. 2/7     15. 7/8
6. 4/9     16. 2/4
7. 3/4     17. 3/5
8. 5/9     18. 1/3
9. 1/3     19. 4/5
10. 4/8

**Page 54**
Check answers to see that the directions have been followed.

**Page 55**
1. 3
2. 2
3. 1
4. 3/9, 3
5. 2/8, 2
6. 3/6
7. 4/6
8. 6/8

**Page 56**
These fractions should be circled:
1. 4/10     6. 4/7
2. 8/10     7. 3/7
3. 2/3      8. 3/4
4. 7/8      9. 3/8
5. 5/9

**Page 57**
1. 4, 3/12
2. 6, 2/12
3. 5, 2/10
4. 8, 1/8
5. 10, 1/10
6. 4, 4/16

**Page 58**
1. 9/100
2. 44/100
3. 98/100
4. 65/100
5. 39/100
6. 27/100
7. 73/100
8. 88/100
9. 23/100
10. 15/100
11. 50/100
12. 11/100
13. <
14. <
15. =
16. >
17. =
18. >

**Page 59**
1. <     7. <
2. <     8. <
3. <     9. >
4. <    10. <
5. >    11. >
6. >

**Page 60**
1. B     7. B
2. A     8. A
3. B     9. B
4. C    10. C
5. C    11. C
6. C    12. A

# This Award
# Is Presented To

_____

## for

★ Doing Your Best

★ Trying Hard

★ Not Giving Up

★ Making a
   Great Effort